100 *Plus* Things

To Do With Your

Grandchildren

A How-To Guide For Grandparents, By Grandparents

Jana Dube Hletko

and

Lynn Zacny Busby

ISBN-13:
978-1976051074

ISBN-10:
197605107X

Cover Design and Interior Layout by Lynn Zacny Busby

Photography by Jana Hletko and Lynn Zacny Busby

Cartoon artists: (reprinted with permission)
Marty Bucella via martybucella.com - pages 58 and 114
Martha Campbell via Cartoonstock.com - page 14

Notice: Every effort has been made to locate the copyright owners of any material used in this book. Please let us know of any error, and we will gladly make any necessary corrections in subsequent printings.

Printed in the United States of America

This book is available through Amazon.com and other fine booksellers.

Table of Contents

Introduction

Grandparents often say: "If we had known how much fun grandchildren are, we would have had them first!" There are bumper stickers, plaques, embroidery kits, and even books proclaiming the attachment grandparents have with their grandchildren. Though children bring parents much joy (and some headaches), there is a very special bond that is possible with grandchildren. It is a relationship built on love, fun, and joy.

Close grandparent/grandchild relationships have healthy benefits. Grandparents can help children flourish. They can offer life wisdom along the way. Since grandparents are free of the daily parenting responsibilities, they have time for uninterrupted play. At times, children may find it easier to talk to a grandparent. Their relationship may help reduce the adverse impacts of some experiences, such as bullying or a divorce in their family.

On the plus side for grandparents, grandchildren can help them feel needed and loved. This can reduce depression according to a study by Boston College researchers.[1]

---

[1] Solidarity in the Grandparent–Adult Grandchild Relationship Sara M. Moorman, PhD Jeffrey E. Stokes, MATHE GERONTOLOGIST, Vol. 56, Issue 3, 1 June 2016, 408–420, 06 June 2014

As a matter of fact, studies show that emotionally close ties between grandparents and their adult grandchildren can reduce rates of depression in BOTH groups.

Involvement with grandchildren can help keep grandparents mentally sharp. Grandparents can benefit from a connection with a much younger generation. They can be exposed to different ideas as their grandchildren navigate through grade school, high school and beyond.

Grandparents love to spoil their grandchildren, and that is not just with material things. Spending time with grandparents can give their grandchildren the feeling that they are the center of attention. It is a wonderful feeling to know you are special.

And, if they start to cry or act badly, they can return to their own homes!

So…. babysit. Share family stories. Sing songs, bake cookies, and visit bookstores. Play games. Wipe some tears. Listen carefully.

MAKE MEMORIES.

Though authors Lynn and Jana have lived in different cities since they were college roommates, they have always kept in close touch and shared their lives. They have visited each other countless times and always find that their friendship simply takes off right where they left off. Though they hate to admit that they could be this old, they have known each other for more than 50 years! They have shared all the wonderful and not so wonderful things that have happened in those years. One of the things they have spent hours talking about has been their grandchildren.

Lynn and Jana have both loved spending time with their grandchildren and have developed many strategies for sharing positive time together. Lynn's grandchildren live near her; that has the huge advantage that they can spend just a few hours together and get together more often. Jana's grandchildren live far away. While she has always considered that a disadvantage, she has worked hard so they can spend positive time together.

A few years ago, Jana wrote *Cousins Camp: A Guide to Spending Special Time With Your Grandchildren* after much encouragement from Lynn. That book is a guide for grandparents who have several days to spend at one time though some of the ideas are appropriate for shorter time spans.

Jana and her husband Paul have nine grandchildren. Lynn and her husband Bob have seven grandchildren. Soooooo, between them, they have 16 grandchildren. They range in age from 4-23. Now, if you add those years together, that totals 824 bazillion grand-parenting years. Well, that may not be accurate, but they do have a good deal of grand-parenting experience. While they have both done their share of babysitting, they have done many different things through the years to cement positive relationships.

This book is intended to give grandparents lots of ideas for things to do with their grandchildren whether they have a few hours or a few days. Grandparents can develop "grandparent block" when they are deciding what to do when their grandchildren arrive. Some of the ideas and activities included in this book are variations of things you may have thought of or done already; they will serve as reminders as you plan. You will find lots of new things to do. Jana and Lynn offer you their many years of experience.

Use this book like a cookbook: Sample an activity from the museum section, sample an activity from the games section, and skip the craft section entirely if it isn't something you enjoy. Reading something on one of their lists may trigger an idea for you.

Activities are divided into INDOORS (kitchen, craft room, game room), OUTDOORS (pool/beach, yard/garden, games), ON THE GO (an afternoon out/a field trip, an overnight excursion).

Most of the activities will be appropriate for children ages 3-14, but you will find that many of them can be adapted to some teens. After all, you know your grandchildren and will be able to pick and choose the activities you will enjoy together.

The most important advice is HAVE FUN.

"I hope my grandma doesn't find out the world doesn't revolve around me."

INDOORS

In the Kitchen

Make dinner together

Teach how to measure, mix, etc. Use an easy recipe. More than likely, you have some family favorite recipes that could be easily adapted so a grandchild can help you cook. Also check out spatulatta.com. This is a cooking-for-kids web site with lots of fun recipes, including dinner, lunch, and vegetarian ideas. Of course, you could order from one of the food delivery services like Blue Apron.

Grands Mini Pizzas

(recipe from Pillsbury Grands Biscuit package)

Ingredients

1) 16.3 ounce can of Pillsbury Grands Refrigerated Biscuits

1 cup pizza sauce

2 cups shredded mozzarella cheese

1 3.5 ounce package sliced pepperoni

1. Press each biscuit into 6-inch round. Place on 2 large or 3 small greased cookie sheets. Top each round with pizza sauce, cheese and pepperoni.

2. Bake at 375 degrees F 10 to 15 minutes or until bottoms are deep golden brown and cheese is bubbly.

Bake together

Christmas cut-out cookies

The month between Thanksgiving and Christmas is a great time to bake Christmas cookies. You can use your own favorite cookie recipe or try some of the slice and bake cookies available at holiday times. That way, your time can be spent decorating.

Lynn uses the Sugar Cookie recipe found on the inside label of Crisco®.

Ultimate Sugar Cookie Recipe

1 stick Crisco® Baking Sticks Butter Flavor All-Vegetable Shortening

OR 1 cup Crisco® Butter Flavor All-Vegetable Shortening

1 cup sugar

1 large egg

2 tablespoons milk

1 tablespoon vanilla extract

3 cups Pillsbury BEST™ All Purpose Flour

1 1/2 teaspoons baking powder

1/2 teaspoon salt

Step one

BEAT shortening and sugar in large bowl with mixer on medium speed until smooth and creamy. Beat in egg, milk and vanilla until well blended.

Step two

COMBINE flour, baking powder and salt in medium bowl. Gradually add to shortening mixture on low speed until blended. Divide dough into three pieces. Wrap in plastic wrap. Chill *(at least)* 1 hour.

Step three

HEAT oven to 375°F. Roll 1 piece of dough at a time on lightly floured surface to 1/8-inch thickness. Cut dough with 2 to 3-inch floured cookie cutters. Place 1-inch apart on ungreased baking sheets.

Step four

BAKE 5 to 9 minutes or until edges begin to brown. Cool 2 minutes. Remove to wire rack to cool completely. Decorate as desired.

Hint: Make the dough the day ahead because it needs to be refrigerated and is ready as needed. The kids will enjoy rolling out the dough and using cookie cutters as much as decorating. Be sure to spread some flour on the board to keep from sticking. An adult should handle getting the cookies in and out of the oven for safety sake.

Icing

Ingredients: powdered sugar and water. One bag of powdered sugar should be sufficient.

That's all there is to it. Put the powdered sugar into a custard cup (fill about half full) and gradually add water – remember the food coloring is going to add moisture so be careful not to make it too runny. If needed, add more powdered sugar to make it thicker.

Mix up the icing and make different colors in small bowls with simple food coloring and have a box of various "sprinkles." The favorite shape is always a Christmas tree. Once they are cooled, the younger kids "paint" the trees with green icing with a pastry brush and add sprinkles. The older kids liked more intricate designs like reindeer, Santa Claus and gingerbread men. Suggestion: Buy tubes of colored icing with decorator tips for them to use for the finer details. Play a radio station with Christmas music in the background to set the mood.

Emilie decorating cookies

The first year Lynn did this she overheard one of the older girls say, "This is really fun!" which is music to a Grandma's ear.

This whole process keeps the grandma very busy – Breaking out small amounts of dough from the refrigerator (keep the bulk in the frig to help it from getting sticky) – filling up the flour bowl, -- filling up the icing bowls, -- putting cookies in the oven, -- taking cookies out of the oven, -- and putting sheets on cooling racks. Suggestion: Use parchment paper to help keep the flow going – you can add the cut out dough to a sheet of parchment paper while the cookie sheets are cooling.

Liz, Emilie, and Katie proud of their finished product

Strawberry Pie

After a trip to the strawberry patch, the apple orchard, or the blueberry field, bake a pie.

> 1 pint fresh strawberries
>
> 1 cup sugar
>
> 1 cup water
>
> 3 TBSP cornstarch
>
> 4 TBSP strawberry Jello
>
> 1 baked pie shell... cooked and cooled (Use your favorite recipe or take a shortcut and use refrigerated pie crust from the grocery store.)
>
> Chocolate kisses (or can use Hershey's Chocolate Bar)

Place chocolate kisses in pie pan with slight space between kisses. Bake at 350 degrees JUST until chocolate melted. Spread.

Arrange cleaned and sliced berries in pie shell.

In saucepan, cook cornstarch, sugar, and water until thick and clear.

Stir in Jello until dissolved.

Pour over strawberries. Chill until ready to serve. Can serve with dollop of whipping cream or Cool Whip.

-----reprinted with permission from Jana's friend and neighbor Kirby Johnstone

Instead of a pie, you can **Make Freezer Jam**. Or, of course, you could do both. Jana has made blueberry jam, blackberry jam and strawberry jam and always uses the recipe found in the Sure-Jell package. NOTE: You will probably find Sure-Jell next to the canning jars and supplies in your grocery store----not in the pudding/Jello section.

Easy Strawberry Jam Recipe

(based on Sure-Jell package directions)

1 Box Sure-Jell Pectin

2 Cups strawberries, crushed

4 Cups white sugar

6 (8 oz.) Ball Jars (cleaned with soap and water)

Clean the fruit. You can place fruit in a big bowl of water or right in the sink. This is a perfect step for little ones.

Remove green tops of berries. Put about one cup at a time in a mixing bowl. Smash the berries with a pastry blender or potato masher. Kids love doing this. You can use an electric blender but the jam will have fewer chunks. You need only 2 cups of smashed berries.

Measure 4 cups of sugar in a separate bowl. Be exact.
Mix the strawberries and the sugar. It will be grainy.

Add 3/4 cup water to a sauce pan and mix it with one box of Sure-Jell pectin. Stir on high heat until it comes to a boil. Boil for one minute stirring continually. The mixture will look a little more clear.

Remove from the stove and immediately add it to the strawberry sugar mixture. Stir for three minutes continually. It becomes very smooth. If there are still a few sugar grains, that's OK.

Fill the 8 oz. jars carefully, leaving 1/2 inch at the top to allow for expansion. If you have a funnel, that will keep things neater. Carefully wipe down all the rims to make sure there is no strawberry on them.

Let the jars sit for 24 hours at room temperature. They should start to set right away. After the 24 hours, place the jars in the freezer. They will last for up to one year in the freezer.

Caramel Brownies

(These are the best brownies ever, and the kids can open all those caramels.)

>1 box German Chocolate Cake mix
>
>½ c. butter, melted
>
>1/3 c. evaporated milk
>
>1 c. chopped pecans

Mix together. Divide the batter in half. Press ½ the mixture in a 9 x 13 GREASED baking pan. Bake at 350 for 7-10 minutes.

>1 pkg. (50) caramels
>
>1/3 c. evaporated milk
>
>Melt together in double boiler or microwave.
>
>Pour on prepared crust.
>
>6 oz. chocolate chips

Layer over caramels. Crumble remaining cake mixture on top. Bake at 375 for 12-15 minutes. Cool. Jana suggests refrigerating the brownies for a while just to firm up the brownies but serve at room temperature. Sprinkle with powdered sugar, if desired.[2]

---

[2] *Based on recipe from Tempting Trios, A Collection of Recipes tested by the Lucile B. Conger Alumnae Group 1988*
Other sources call these brownies Best Brownies Ever, Knock Your Socks Off Brownies, or several other titles.

Make a multi-color cake

Use your favorite cake and frosting recipe OR take a shortcut and use a box cake and canned buttercream frosting.

Ingredients:

> Yellow (or white) cake batter
>
> Gel food dye
>
> Buttercream frosting

Follow the box cake directions or prepare your cake batter.

Divide into however many sections that you would like. If you don't want to make a layer cake, just use a sheet cake pan.

Use food dye to color the cake batter. Gel or paste may need only 1 drop per section for a bright color. Food coloring drops may need more. McCormick Neon Food Color would be a fun choice. You want the colors to be bright.

Drop your batter by dollops into the pan one color at a time and bake as normal. Don't mix the colors.

5. Let cake cool and frost. Sprinkle with colored sprinkles. There are classic jimmies, confetti sprinkles, and sprinkle blends.

Squeeze orange juice for breakfast

This old-fashioned activity is really fun for children. With today's busy schedules, it is doubtful that they have done this with their parents.

Grow a plant from an avocado seed

1. Remove and clean the pit. (Peel away the brown covering.)
2. Decide which end is the top and which is the bottom (bottom will be more rounded). The top will sprout and should be kept dry.
3. Pierce with three to four toothpicks around the seed.
4. Submerge the bottom half of the seed in a glass of water.
5. When the seed sprouts, (30-90) days), leave one new shoot at the top and pinch off the rest of the new growth.

This is a great activity if your grandchild lives close by, and you can monitor the growth of your plant.

Host a theme night

French night 2016

When the Hletkos have the whole family for several days in a row, they make dinner easier by ordering in and using paper plates. To make it a special occasion, they have had Upside Down Birthday Night, Valentines Night, Hawaiian Night, Italian Night, Irish Night, Mexican Night, Baseball Night (Cubs one year, Washington Nationals the next year), French Night, Western Night, Mardi Gras Night, Carnival Night (complete with carnival games). NOTE: You can read more about these theme nights in *Cousins Camp, 2.0* (Amazon.com). The children help with putting out the decorations and setting the table.

Chase the pepper

This is a cool trick your grandchild will want to share with everyone. Fill a pie plate with water. Shake out some pepper on the water. Now put a piece of wet soap in the pie plate. The pepper runs away from the soap! If you shake some sugar into the clear area, the pepper will come back.

Shuck corn

Kids will think this is fun if it is done as a group activity. Hint: Lay down newspaper on a table or have them sit on some outside steps to cut down on the mess.

Make a gingerbread house

Though she hasn't done this with grandchildren, Jana and her children made a house every year. They started from scratch, making the gingerbread and then decorating it. As she recalls, everyone started out enthusiastically, but by the end of the project she seemed to be alone! The good news is that you can now buy a kit at your local grocery store and just do the fun decorating.

In the Craft Room

(In Lynn and Jana's homes, the craft room is the kitchen! It becomes the craft room when they put a protective covering on the kitchen table. **NOTE**: Yes, that is a tip Jana learned AFTER she noticed the acrylic paint stain on her kitchen table.)

Mosaic pictures

The big advantage of this craft is that there are different levels of difficulty. Therefore, young children can work on their own picture right beside their older siblings. These are available at craft stores, toy stores, and, of course, Amazon.

Sabine, 2017

Make a pretend hot air balloon

If you don't have a real one near by (or prefer to keep your feet on the ground) you can put together a pretend hot air balloon with a laundry basket and some helium balloons.

Make a Halloween costume

Lynn enjoys sewing and making costumes. She works with each grandchild to plan the costume together and have a couple of "fittings" before Halloween. The grandchild picks out what they want to "be" and then she puts her creative juices to work to figure out a way to design it. They especially like having a "unique" favorite character costume rather than a store-bought one. If you don't sew, you can still make some unique items with stick-on Velcro.

Once you know who/what they want to be you can start collecting things to use with the costume. Thrift stores and garage sales are great places to find low cost fabric and/or props for the costumes.

Jules, Katie, Liz, Natalie, Nick, Logan Halloween costumes over the years

Pottery painting

This can be done in your own home using a kit purchased from a craft or toy store, or you could go to one of the Paint Your Own type stores such as Color Me Mine.

If you elect to go to a local store, the kids can pick out white pottery items (of course, the grandparent pays!). The kids paint the pottery; the pottery is then baked in a kiln for pickup in a day or two. Lynn took her grandkids to her local store to make a present for their moms for Mother's Day.

Perler Beads

These are guaranteed to provide hours of fun. Caution: an adult is needed to iron the final creations. The beads can be purchased at craft stores or amazon.com.

Woodworking

If you have these skills, it would be wonderful to make a small table, a step stool, or a basic dollhouse.

Crocheting, Knitting

Older kids have the coordination to learn knitting or crocheting. If you don't know how yourself, there are usually local adult education classes offering lessons. Make a simple item like a potholder and have them work on it during down time or while watching TV. They will love being able to take home a gift. You can find a "Free Crochet Pattern for Easy Afghan Stitch Potholders" by Amy Solovay on the Spruce Website: https://www.thespruce.com/afghan-stitch-potholders-978948

Paint with shaving cream

Use non-mint foam (gel won't work). Keep out of eyes. You can use acrylic paint, but remember that it stains. Use food coloring instead.

Use thick white paper like card stock.

Squirt shaving cream all over a baking sheet (with edges).

Spread the cream over the baking sheet in a smooth, thick layer.

Drip food coloring all over the shaving cream.

Using a chopstick or wooden skewer, swirl the colors through the shaving cream. Don't over-mix or you will have one color!

Gently press the paper on the surface of the shaving cream. Let it rest for a bit......30 seconds should do it.

Lift the paper carefully out of the shaving cream.

Using a sturdy object with a straight edge (think tongue depressor, ruler, piece of cardboard), scrape over the surface of the paper to remove the shaving cream. Voila! You have a lovely piece of marbleized paper.

Use the paper for a card... or a picture frame...or the cover for a journal.

Create a homemade band

Kids love to make music... and noise. Instruments don't have to be expensive. Have them make some homemade instruments and then march down the street playing their favorite song (e.g. Twinkle Twinkle Little Star, The Wheels on the Bus, etc.).

How to make instruments:

Comb kazoo

Measure out a piece of wax paper that is as long as your comb and 2 times as wide. Hold the comb with the teeth pointing down and fold the wax paper around the comb to cover both sides. Hold the paper lightly against the comb. Place the paper and comb lightly against your lips and hum your favorite tune.

You could also make a different kazoo sound by stretching the wax paper over a toilet paper roll and securing with a rubber band – then blow into it.

Whisk maraca

Squeeze a jingle bell into a kitchen whisk and you have a great tinkling maraca.

Drums

Kids love to beat on anything. Use a wooden spoon for a mallet and an old pot or cookie sheet for the drum. Use anything that will be easy to carry and beat on at the same time.

Guiro shaker

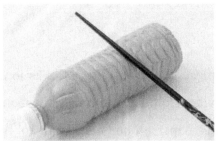

Fill an empty plastic bottle with unpopped corn or uncooked rice and screw the lid on tight. Voila: you have a nice rumba shaker sound. Ideally, the bottle will have a rippled body so a stick (a chop stick works perfectly) can be drawn across the ripples for a different sound like a quiro.

Water bottle tuba

Start with an empty, clean plastic bottle. Fill it about half way full with water. Hold the bottle upright (so it is perpendicular to your face) and blow across the top of the bottle to make a resonant sound. Touch your lower lip to the edge of the bottle, pursing your upper lip and blowing gently over the opening. When you get the angle and airflow just right, you will hear a musical note as the air column in the open bottle resonates.

There are many more ideas on the web – search for "homemade band instruments."

Color eggs

Coloring eggs is a fun activity for the whole family around Easter time. The adults can share fancy techniques such as making striped eggs; young ones enjoy putting stickers on the colored eggs.

Logan and Nick coloring eggs

Make no-sew dog toys

Make some no-sew dog toys for your family dogs or the animals in shelters using inexpensive fleece remnants or old torn jeans. If you don't have any, they can be found in most thrift stores. Cut into strips, braid, and tie in knots for an easy tug or throw toy.

Decorate Christmas ornaments

Start with plain colored ornaments and decorate them or make your own.

Make pipe cleaner ornaments

An easy make-your-own requires only some pipe cleaners and beads. String the beads on the pipe cleaners and then bend them into Christmas shapes (bells, stars, angels, etc.)

Logan making pipe cleaner ornaments

Make salt dough Christmas ornaments

Ingredients

> 4 cups flour
> 1 cup salt
> 1.5 cups water

Mix together, adding more flour and water in small amounts until right consistency. It shouldn't be sticky but can't be too dry. Roll out dough. Have kids put handprints in dough, and then cut out into circle. NOTE: Don't forget to leave a hole for string to hang the ornament. Bake for 20 min at 350F. Paint to decorate. You could add food coloring for colored dough. Instead of an ornament, the hand print can be a paperweight. Just don't leave a hole for the string.

Make a special Christmas "bag" or stocking

Make a special gift wrapper with each child's name on it and use it every year with a new gift in it. The kids look forward to their special gift in their very own bag/stocking.

Katie, 2003

Make your own play dough

Ingredients

4 cups flour
1 cup salt
1½ cup water, warm
3 -5 drops of natural food coloring

Instructions

1. Mix together flour and salt.

2. Mix water with a few drops of food coloring.

3. Slowly pour the water into the flour mixture, stirring as you pour. Stir until combined; mix with your hands until the flour is completely absorbed. If the dough is too sticky, add more flour.

4. Add glitter for fun.

Make puppets and put on a show

One year Jana purchased cute puppet sets for Cousins Camp. Then the next year, she had wooden spoon puppets that were much cheaper. Of course, you can use old socks, yarn, and buttons and put your own puppets together. Write a brief play together and let the children perform. Take a short movie and send it to their parents.

Andrew and Sofie showing off puppets, 2014

Have an art party

The high school art teacher where Jana used to teach will come to your home. The costs are quite reasonable; she brings all the supplies, including table-sized easels that the kids thought were wonderful. They had a choice of things they could paint. As you see, they chose the octopus. Though they did not have any wine that may have been part of an adult party, they had a great time. Call your local schools to see if someone is doing this near you.

(back) Andrew, Audrey, Ellie, Sabine (front) Eloise, Lucille 2017

Make your own picture soap

Though making soap is complicated, you can decorate purchased bars of soap and still have a personalized product.

You will need:

> Bar of soap
>
> Glue
>
> Photo or other picture from magazine
>
> Canning wax
>
> Small empty can
>
> Pan of hot water
>
> Paintbrush

Glue a photo or picture onto a bar of soap. Melt canning wax in a small empty can in a pan of hot water. *CAUTION: ADULT SUPERVISION IS MANDATORY.*

Dip a paintbrush in the melted wax and "paint" it over the picture. This will waterproof the picture. This is fun for bathtub soap or the child can give it as a present. Think Mothers Day.

Make an EASY bird feeder

Tie a string around the top of a pinecone (under the ridges). Knot the string but leave enough string to hang it on a tree outside. Cover the pinecone with peanut butter. Roll it in birdseed.

Make a scrapbook of your adventures

Be sure to take pictures of your activities, adventures. Then put them all together in a scrapbook or album of some type. Pages could be written about the art of scrapbooking, but you can do something simpler that doesn't require all the supplies of scrapbooking. Snapfish, Shutterfly, IBook, WalMart Photo all will help you put great albums together. You can make this a yearly project or any time period that is appropriate for your activities.

Cover:

Inside pages:

Make your own puzzle

You can use old magazines or family photos. Just cut out pictures from magazines or blow up a picture of your grandchild. Glue the picture on to a piece of cardboard. No cardboard should show. Then, cut the picture into pieces and let your grandchild put the pieces back together. It would be fun to have pictures of different members of the family. The picture pieces could then be put together in a pile, making it more difficult to put the people back together.

Decorate using shells

Plain jars can be decorated easily with shells. Fill your jars with sand and then wrap raffia, ribbon, or twine around the jar tops. Tuck in a starfish and tie on sand dollars, shells, and other various beach treasures. You can hot glue the ends of the ribbon, etc. inside a shell.

You could also make a stepping-stone using your shells. You can either buy a kit or make your own. The Better Home and Gardens web site has clear, easy directions for a child's stepping-stone. You can find it at bhg.com

Trace your genealogy

Some kids are interested in their heritage. If you have one who shows interest, sign up for Ancestry.com. You can get a "guest account" which gives you access to their free databases and allows you to build a tree.

This is a great way to get kids to document what you know about your family tree. Sometimes people don't get interested in their heritage until the people who hold the memories are gone. Help them document their family tree and tell some favorite stories about your relatives along the way. All kids love to hear stories about their parents/grandparents as kids.

Note: Ancestry.com is a subscription service, but one of Ancestry's best-kept secrets is that they also have almost 2000 free databases. To view these free records, you may be asked to sign up for an account, but the account is free. Fees are required to access the entire set of databases.

Note: Lynn is putting together a book on the evolution of the DePriest family in America; she has compiled almost 400 pages. She has discovered original documentation on the first DePriest

immigrant, a French Huguenot dating to the late 17th century, as well as many other old documents that are included. There are thousands of DePriest descendents in America including her line. Her book should be helpful to others researching their own families.

She has found relatives who served in the Revolutionary War, making history more meaningful to her grandchildren. The old photos of family members she has discovered have made that history much more interesting.

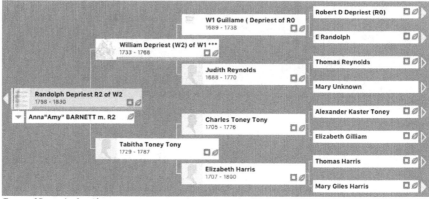

Part of Lynn's family tree

Share family folk lore

Tell your grandchild a family story about when their parents were young. They will want to hear these over and over. Don't give away any parent secrets though!

Get out your family photo albums

Lynn is the baby with her mother and brothers (Gary, Bob, and Jim)

Your grandchildren will love seeing their parents/grandparents growing up. Think of the laughter when they see the clothes, hairstyles, and shoes that their parents thought were so cool. This is a great opportunity to connect grandchildren to their past.

Create a family book

Put together a family book with pictures of each family member. Add some basic information about each one: birthday, birthplace, parents, siblings, and favorite things.

Two of the pages about Jana in the books she made for her grandchildren

Page about Jana's husband, Paul

In the Game Room

(The game room can sometimes be the kitchen, sometimes the living room, and sometimes the dining room. It just depends on the activity. If you have a separate game room, you will enjoy sharing it with your grandchildren.)

Play Monopoly, Clue, jacks, marbles, dominoes, chess...

Grandpa and Ellie 2017

Basic rules for Dominoes:

It may have been awhile since you played dominoes so here is a quick cheat sheet reminder:

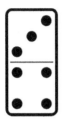 **To start:** Put all the dominoes face down on a table. Mix them up. Each player takes 7 dominoes. Don't let your opponent see your dominoes.

The first player should be the one with the highest double tile. Put the tile on the table (right side up) to begin.

To play: The player to the left places a matching domino next to the first one. So…. If the first player started the game with a double six, the next player has to play a domino with a six on it. Doubles are placed perpendicular when they are played.

The first double played is the "spinner." The spinner may be played off either end as well as its regular sides. The spinner is the only place where it can be played off in 4 ways.

If the player doesn't have a domino they can play, they have to draw a domino from the pile (called the boneyard). They must keep picking up dominoes until they get a domino they can play. If at some point there is no playable domino, then the player has to pass their turn. They "knock" or say pass.

Scoring: Points can be added during the play by making the exposed ends of the chain total to a multiple of five. At the end of each hand, the winner scores points for all the remaining unplayed dominoes in the other player's hands. Add points and round to the nearest multiple of five.

Winner: The first player to reach 150 points wins.

For more dominoes information, visit

http://www.domino-games.com/domino-rules/domino-basics.html

Play Simon Says

Choose one player (probably should be a parent or grandparent for the first round) to be Simon. The rest of the players will line up in front of Simon as he calls out actions starting with the phrase "Simon says": "Simon says…tap your head." The players tap their heads. BUT, if Simon calls out an action without saying "Simon says," the kids must NOT do the action. If they do, they are out of the game. To be tricky, Simon will do something without saying "Simon Says." The last player left in the game wins and becomes the next Simon.

Play pencil and paper games

Today's Parent has a number of games listed on their website, and they provide forms to be downloaded. See https://www.todaysparent.com/toddler/20-fun-indoor-games/

Play Bridge

Many bridge players learned to play bridge when they were quite young because they had a grandparent who needed a partner to play.

Play Rummy

A simpler card game would be Rummy. Of course, there are many variations of the game. If you want to investigate some card games including variations of Rummy, the book *Card Games for Dummies, 2nd Edition* could be helpful. In the meantime, here are some basic directions:

Deal out 10 cards (with 6-11 players, you need 2 decks of cards and then each player gets 7 cards). If you have just 2 players, you could also play with 7 cards each.

The dealer deals out the hands and puts the rest of the cards face down on the center of the table. Turn the top card over so everyone can see it. That will be the first card of the discard pile.

The player to the left of the dealer plays first. She can either pick up the card on the discard pile or she can pick up the top card on the deck. Then, the player must discard one card.

The next player has the choice of picking up the last card from the discard pile or the top card from the deck.

Players are trying to get their cards into two types of combinations: RUNS which are consecutive sequences of three or more cards OF THE SAME SUIT or SETS which are three or four cards of the same rank, such as 4's or Jacks, etc.

You can put down a run or set before you are ready to go out completely, or you can wait until you can go out. Once your cards are on the table, opponents can add to your combinations, which will help them go out quicker. Of course, if you hold your cards until the end, you could get stuck with lots of points in your hand.

You can play that the winner is the low scorer..... when you go out, your opponents have to add up the value of the cards in their hand and that is their score. OR you can play the winner is the high scorer. In that variation, the player who goes out would accumulate the points from the opponents' hands. Decide if you will play to 100 or whatever score you choose.

Play I Doubt It (otherwise known as B.S.!)

"I Doubt It" is a fun card game that's great for children and adults to play together. 3 to 5 players can play with one deck of cards. 6 to 11 players need two decks of cards. Use cards with identical backs if possible so the players cannot tell them apart.

Goal

Be the first to get rid of all your cards.

Setup

Shuffle all the cards together. Deal them out as evenly as possible.

Gameplay

The first player plays one or more cards from his hand, face down, starting a discard pile in the middle of the table. He says, "One Ace," or whatever number is appropriate (i.e. the number of cards he played).

The second player plays one or more cards from his hand, face down, on top of the discard pile. He says, "Two Kings," or whatever number is appropriate (i.e. the number of cards he played).

This continues with each subsequent player moving down one rank -- so the third player would say "Queens," the fourth "Jacks," the fifth "10s," and so on. After a player discards (or claims to discard) 2s, the next player will discard (or claim to discard) Aces. Alternatively, you can start with a low number and work your way up. Decide before you start.

It is perfectly legal, and in fact necessary, for players to sometimes play cards that are not what they say. For example, a player might play a 10 and a 9 but say, "two Queens." The only penalty comes if such a player is caught (see "Doubting," below). Remember, you want to get rid of your cards!

Doubting

After each discard, any other player can say, "I doubt it."

The last player's discarded cards are then turned face up.

If any card in that set is not what the player declared, the player must take the entire discard pile into his hand. If the card(s) is what the discarder claimed, then the doubter has to pick up the entire discard pile.

Note: the first player to say "I Doubt It" is the official doubter. If more than one player says " I Doubt It " at the same time, the player closest to the left of the one who made the discard is the official doubter.

Winning

The first player to get rid of all his cards wins. The last play is always made face up, because other players will inevitably doubt it.

Play I Spy

This quiet game doesn't need any supplies and can be played anywhere. It is a good game to play in the car, too.

To play:
You need at least 2 players. The first person to be the spy decides what they want to select as their object. The other player has to guess what it is based on a series of clues.

The first clue is usually a color. The spy can say, " I spy something with my little eye. It is green." Remember not to say what the object is! If no one guesses correctly, the spy can give another hint. This could be height, the material it is made of, the weight, the texture, the first letter of the word, or a word it sounds like. Be careful if you are playing in the car because you will pass objects quickly.

The player who guesses correctly becomes the next spy.

Play Freeze

Choose some lively music and turn up the volume. Everyone should dance and move to the music. When it stops, they have to freeze no matter what position they are in!

Walk on a balance beam

When you have your music ready, get out some masking tape and mark off a "balance beam" on the floor. Kids can take turns walking a straight line while the music plays. Older kids can walk backwards or balance on one foot.

Play Animal Charades

Make a set of cards with animal pictures on them. You can use drawings that the kids have made, find pictures in magazines, or download a set of Acting Like Animals cards from https://www.nwf.org/kids/family-fun/crafts/animal-charades-matching-game.aspx.

Each player gets one card and acts out the animal while other family members guess what they are. You can add sounds.

Set up a mini casino

A few years ago, Jana's son decided to teach the kids how to play poker and craps! They had a great time. However, she had to admit that she was a little embarrassed when she heard Sofie yell across the community pool to Andrew: "Hey, Andrew! You wanna go home and play craps?"

Lucille, Sofie, Sabine 2016

Learn a new game

Old-fashioned games can be lots of fun. Kids love some of the newer games, also. Some favorites are Happy Salmon, Tensies, Spot It, LRC (Left, Right, Center), and Jenga. Jana's grandchildren love Mancala. It's an old game, but it is new for her. She said it took her a while to get the hang of it, but they loved teaching her a game.

Sabine, patiently teaching Jana to play Mancala, 2017

Have your grandchild teach you tech

The younger generation is very comfortable with technology. You could have your grandchild teach you something about your computer, pad, or smartphone.

You could learn about a software program together. Learn how to use Messaging, Facetime, Instagram, Snapchat, Twitter, etc. If you don't already have a Facebook account, you could set one up so you can keep in touch.

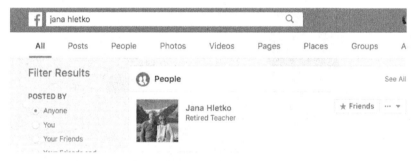

Facebook screen shot for Jana

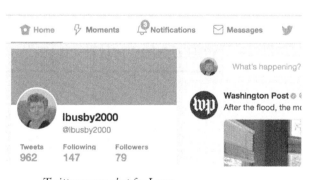

Twitter screen shot for Lynn

"No, grandma, hashtags are not something you order with eggs."

Play Bingo

A few years ago, Jana purchased a Bingo set on Amazon.com with a rotary cage (little balls turn in a cage and one rolls out). Her grandchildren all love this. It is so much more dramatic than just calling out letters from a bag. She keeps a basket filled with small prizes they can pick when they have a Bingo.

HINT: The grandparent should always be the caller; the basket may not stay situated on the stand with an excited grandchild calling out the numbers.

Play hide and seek

An oldie but a goldie –the simplest of games can be fun even in the day of today's video gaming, phone hypnosis, etc.

Put a puzzle together

Natalie with Pop

Start with a puzzle with 50-100 pieces for the younger crowd and work up to 500 piece or even 1,000 piece puzzles. If you would like, you can keep your puzzle together and display it as a piece of art when you are finished. Here's how:

Complete the puzzle. Make sure the pieces fit together nicely.

Using wax paper or parchment paper, slide it under your puzzle. This could take two people. The point here is to make sure no glue will seep onto your table.

Flatten the puzzle completely....a rolling pin would be great here. Pour the glue right over the puzzle. Jana has used SunsOUT puzzle glue, but there are several products that will do the trick. Be sure to spread the glue out evenly. You can use a small piece of cardboard or a plastic knife. Be sure to get some glue on the edges of the puzzle. ONE PIECE OF ADVICE: don't put on too much glue because that will make your puzzle pieces swell and peel. It will be mostly dry in just a couple of hours, but for total drying, wait 4 hours. Of course, follow the directions on your glue product.

Make a time capsule

Include objects that you and your grandchild decide are important such as drawings, letters, and pictures. Mark your capsule with the date you created it and the date you want to revisit it. Bury it in your backyard or place it on a top shelf in your closet. Burying it outdoors creates some complications because you will have to try to keep everything dry. An indoor "burial" may be a better option. Then, mark your phone calendar for the date you want to reopen your capsule.

Make and fly paper airplanes

You can see who can fly their plane the farthest or see who can land their plane more accurately. You may remember how to make a paper airplane; if not, here are a couple of websites that will take you through the process, including explanatory pictures:

http://www.artofmanliness.com/2014/09/16/how-to-make-the-worlds-best-paper-airplanes
or
http://m.wikihow.com/Make-a-Fast-Paper-Airplane

Spin a globe and stick your finger on a spot.

When it stops, research the destination. NOTE: Be sure to use a globe with current country labels.

If your grandchild lives near you, you could subscribe to Little Passports (littlepassports.com) and study a different country each month. Monthly packages arrive with souvenirs and activities. The first month subscription comes with a little suitcase to keep everything together. Of course, the shipment could be sent to the child's home and then you could discuss what they have received when you see each other or talk using Skype or Facetime.

Do a science experiment

You can buy kits at toy stores or online or find experiments on the Internet. If your grandchild lives near you and you are able to get together on a regular basis, you may want to invest in one of the subscription science kits for kids. For example, Tinker Crate and Kiwi Crate send out monthly STEM projects for kids ages 3-16 (www.kwicocom/).

Make up a story

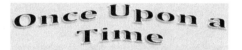

Make up and tell your grandchild a story about a time when they saved the day. This is an abbreviated example: Once upon a time, long long ago, there was a little boy/girl named (insert name here). One day, he/she/they were walking along a beach and suddenly saw a pirate ship coming right to shore. (Name the child) ran to a lifeguard....the lifeguard called the police....the police and fire department screeched into the beach and, using a megaphone, warned the pirates not to come any closer. When the pirate ship turned back out to sea, everyone cheered for the child/children. The mayor declared a (Child) Saves the Day parade for the very next week. The entire city watched as the children rode by in their limousines and received the key to the city. You can extrapolate on this story by adding many details..... pirate with one leg, a parrot, etc. etc. etc.

Watch a movie

Kids will enjoy some of the old favorites: Singing in the Rain ,
all the Disney films, Yankee Doodle Dandy, etc. Movies are
easily accessed through Netflix or other subscription services.

Cousins watching Madagascar together: Natalie, Katie, Jules, Logan, Liz

Build a fort

Use blankets and pillows or old cardboard boxes. Drape the
blankets over chairs and couches to make a cozy place.

Declare an Upside Down Day

Though Jana's family celebrated a whole Upside Down Birthday at Cousins Camp a couple of years ago, you can declare any day an Upside Down Day. In the morning, say "good night," wear some clothing inside out, eat dessert before dinner. At night, say "good morning." Be creative.

Andrew, left, and PQ, right 2016
Since Andrew (left) had his underwear on top of his shorts, his mother asked him if he had underwear on UNDER the shorts. His answer: "You may not want to know."

Have an "olden days" dress up day

One year Lynn made poodle skirts for the girl cousins for a 50s theme party.

Natalie, Jules, Liz, Katie, 2011

Play Pass the Bag

Fill a big garbage bag with different clothing items. If you don't have enough old clothes in your closets to use for this game, a quick trip to a second-hand store should solve the problem. You can include shoes, purses, scarves, hats, socks, shirts, skirts, and pants. Everyone should stand in a circle and pass the bag around while music plays. (Think of this as a variation of Musical Chairs.) When the music stops, the person holding the bag must reach into the bag and pull out one item. Peeking into the bag is against the rules. The player then puts on the item. Keep going until the bag is empty and everyone is dressed in ridiculous outfits. You will want pictures of this one.

Play Musical Chairs or the Lap Game

The Lap Game

You can adapt the questions to fit your group.

Directions:

Arrange furniture in a circle and have everyone take a seat.

Say: I'm going to ask everyone a series of questions. If you can answer yes to the question, I want you to move one seat to your left. If you cannot answer yes to the question, I want you to stay where you are. As you can imagine, if you have done what I have asked, but the person to your left has not, you are going to have to share a seat. So get ready to be comfortable with each other.

The first person to make it back to their original seat wins the prize!

1. Have you ever been on an airplane?
2. Have you ever been in a car stopped by police?
3. Have you ever told a white lie to avoid hurting someone's feelings?
4. Have you ever returned a gift and exchanged it for something else?
5. Have you ever re-gifted something?
6. Have you ever left the USA? (e.g. Canada, Mexico, Europe)
7. Have you ever done something you did not want to do.....and realized it was fun?

8. Have you ever cried while you were watching a movie?

9. Have you ever laughed so hard that milk… or something…. shot out of your nose?

10. Have you ever done something your parents said you couldn't do?

11. Have you ever forgotten something at home…. And your parent had to bring it to you?

12. Have you ever tried playing a sport you didn't like?

13. Have you ever read more than one book in a week?

14. Have you ever cried…. Or laughed out loud when you were reading a book?

15. Have you ever had fun at Cousins Camp?

Players look on as Ellie and Eloise decide how to sit on the chair together.

Complete a yearly questionnaire

Develop a questionnaire and have the child(ren) fill it out one time per year. If your family all gathers at July 4, Thanksgiving, Christmas, New Years or some other specific time, use that time. Then save the questionnaires. In just a few years, you will be able to share them with each other. It should make for some frivolity....or at least a chance to share some nice memories.

Sample : (fill in the year)

My 20xx Questionnaire   Name: _____

My favorite color   _____

My favorite book _____

My favorite food _____

My favorite game _____

My best friend(s) _____

My favorite teacher _____

Two things I did that I loved!

1.   _____

2.   _____

Something I am looking forward to in 20xx

_____

What I want to be when I grow up

_____

Make a toy area in your home

Have a special area or make a toy box where you keep toys at
your house. They always go straight for the toy box and look
forward to going to Grandma's house knowing there is
something special waiting for them.

Natalie – first stop: the Toybox

Make balloon animals

Balloons for this activity are long and skinny and typically come
with a plastic hand pump to blow them up and a manual for how
to make different animals.

OUTDOORS

NOTE: Remember sunscreen.

Yard/Garden/Park

Go bird watching

(See Bird Feeder under Arts and Crafts.) If you know about birds, teach what you know...if not, get a bird identification book and discover different species together.

There is an excellent program (but costs $) for an IPhone called Bird Explorer that helps to identify birds with various information about them, including their sounds.

iBird Pro Guide to Birds

Ratings: ★ ★ ★ ★ ½ (4168)
Version: **10.01**
Database Size: **1587MB**

iBird Pro contains 944 species of North American birds, including both common and rare species. It is designed to help both experienced and novice birders identify and learn about their birds.

Rake leaves

If you live in a home with a lot of trees, let the grandkids rake and play in leaves. Lynn puts down a plastic drop cloth. Then, they rake the leaves and pile them on the drop cloth. Jumping in a pile of leaves is still fun.

After the leaves get smashed down, they pick up the cloth and carry the leaves and dump them in the back/common ground area and start all over. If you don't back up to common ground, hold a yard waste bag for them to dump the leaves in. Yes, this smacks of Tom Sawyer.

Blow big bubbles

This is a combination craft room and outdoor activity. There are lots of recipes available; the following is one of the easier ones.

Ingredients

> 11 c. water
> 4 c. Ajax dish soap (not antibacterial)
> 1 c. corn syrup

Steps

In a clean plastic container, combine ingredients and mix well. Tip: Dirt and other contaminants can ruin the solution.

For the wand, use a child's toy tennis racket with the netting cut out. Dip wand in solution and wave slowly. Works best on humid, cloudy days.

Wash your car

You may have to remind them that washing the wheels is an honorary post. You will need a car-wash product, sponge or lamb's wool mitt, nonabrasive cloth for road tar deposits, wheel cleaner or mild soap and water. For specific directions, go to consumerreports.org.

Fly a kite (store bought or make your own)

Make a paper bag kite

You will need:

> a large paper bag
>
> a hole punch
>
> paper ring reinforcements
>
> scissors
>
> string
>
> paint or makers
>
> a stapler or glue
>
> crepe paper streamers

Punch a hole on each of the 4 corners of the bag.... one inch from edge of bag.

Reinforce hole with the paper ring reinforcements.

Cut two 3 foot lengths of string and tie each end to a hole...... form 2 loops.

Cut another three 3 foot length of string.

Tie it through the two loops, creating a handle.

Decorate the bag with paint or markers.

Glue or staple some crepe paper streamers on the bag.

Hold the kite.... And run!

Look for pirate's treasure

If you have a sandbox, you are ready for this one. If you don't, you can fill a plastic bin with play sand. Of course, if you live near the beach, you have sand readily available.

Before your grandchild arrives, bury a few small toys or trinkets in the sand. Small dinosaurs, plastic jewelry, a few coins, and little cars would all be perfect. Then, let your grandchild dig for treasure using small plastic shovels or rakes.

Go for a walk

Help the kids identify trees on your route. Talk about the different cloud shapes. Stop and smell the roses!

Make it a Scavenger Hunt. Look for objects that begin with the letters of your last name or the city where you live.

Set up a lemonade stand

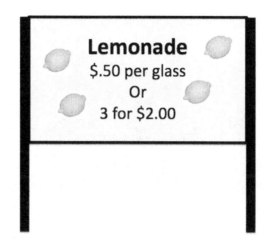

A few years ago, one of Jana's neighbors helped her grandchildren set up a stand and even included cookies for sale. Jana laughed when she saw the sign they made: LEMONADE 50 Cents 3 glasses $2.00 Most customers probably bought just one glass! That family will have a lasting memory of that day.

Have a picnic

You can go to a park, your own backyard, or even your living room in case of rain. Food tastes better when it comes out of a picnic basket.

Pool/Beach/Lake

Walk on a beach and collect seashells

Cousins at the beach 2014

This can be a combination outdoor and craft item.

There are many crafts you can work on once you have accumulated your beautiful shells. See the craft section for two ideas.

Build a sandcastle

This can be very simple for young children or a work of art for the older kids. You will need buckets, shovels, rakes. HINT: have at least one sturdy shovel rather than the small plastic ones that are sold with sand buckets.

Get out on a lake

Consider the possibilities: rowboat, canoe, sailboat, fishing, and swimming. This is a summer imperative.

Pop with Jules and Liz at Forest Park, St. Louis, MO

Jules and Liz before paddle boat trip

Go fishing

If you don't have access to a lake, try "fishing" in your back yard.

Logan
fishing on dry dock

Go to a park or lake and feed the ducks

(Check to make sure feeding is allowed.)

Ducks are usually friendly and happy to scrounge for food. Note: Beware of geese; they can get mean.

Hunt for mushrooms in the woods

Jana's dad knew every kind of mushroom.... and could keep them away from the poisonous ones! Don't attempt this if you don't know what you are doing.

Outdoor Games

Play a game involving water

Here are four possibilities:

Wet and freeze 2 t-shirts

(or 3 depending on the number of people on each team)
Remove shirts from freezer and give one to each team. The 1st team to get a shirt on to their team leader WINS.

Relay race

You will need a LARGE sponge and 2 buckets per team
1st person in line wets sponge, passes it overhead to person behind him.....continue to end of line. Last person squeezes out water into bucket behind him and runs to front of line. Use a smaller bucket at end of the line. This could also be done in a swimming pool.

Balloon toss:

Fill balloons with water.....the number of balloons will determine how long the game lasts. One child tosses a balloon to another child. Place them in lines facing each other. When the balloon bursts, that child is out. Game continues until one child is remaining.

Water gun target shooting

Set up some targets, fill the water guns, and stay out of the way.

Nick and Logan

Play Wiffle ball

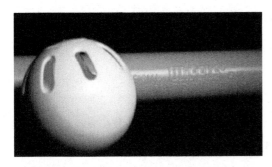

The great thing about Wiffle ball is that no one gets hurt – even if some of the fielders aren't paying attention to the game.

Play hopscotch

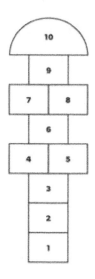

Use sidewalk chalk to draw the outline for your game. If you don't remember how to play, see kidspot.com.au. NOTE: This is a game that might be better left to younger grandparents! But everyone can enjoy designing flowers, plants, animals, etc. on the sidewalk. Clean up is easy….. just wait for the rain to clean it up!

Play beanbag toss

Though there are commercial games available, it would be pretty simple to make your own game. First, make some beanbags with rice or beans. You can sew some basic beanbags or use zip-lock bags. Then, flowerpot saucers can be used for the targets. Just place them in a line with the farthest one being worth the most points.

ON THE GO

NOTE: If you are planning to travel with a grandchild, be sure to have appropriate car seat/seat belt rules. A car seat can turn out to be a good investment and will save you the trouble of transferring a car seat from the parent's car to your car every time you want to go somewhere.

An Afternoon Out/A Field Trip

Pick fruit

Go pick apples, strawberries, or blueberries (see strawberry pie recipe on page 21)

Nick and Logan

Have a yearly 1:1 birthday lunch

The grandchild picks the location for his or her birthday. Only the birthday child goes with the grandparents leaving any siblings behind and making the birthday lunch/dinner just for their special day.

One restaurant Lynn and Bob went to had a feather boa for the birthday girl; another had a Chinese parade complete with drums and dragon in costume for the birthday boy.

Play miniature golf

Miniature golf is great fun for all ages. Or if your grandchildren are old enough, play golf.

Go ice skating or roller skating

This will probably be a spectator sport for most grandparents, but it is fun to watch the kids excel or struggle and lend a comforting ear if/when someone falls.

Get a manicure / pedicure together

Be sure to pick a salon that is child friendly.

Visit your local library or a bookstore

Besides books, libraries provide multiple activities. Local libraries have worked hard to be attractive. Jana's local library has craft events, game nights, Lego play, a manners class, and an opportunity to read to a dog.

Or go to a local bookstore. There are still fabulous bookstores.

A few bookstores that cater to children include:

A Children's Place	Portland, Oregon
Bank Street Books	New York, New York
Vroman's Bookstore	Los Angeles, California
Blue Marble Books	Fort Thomas, Kentucky
Blue Manatee Bookstore	Cincinnati, Ohio
Blue Willow Bookstore	Houston, Texas
Brattle Book Shop	Boston, Massachusetts
Ellliott Bay Book Company	Seattle, Washington
The Reading Bug	San Carlos, California
The Little Shop of Stories	Atlanta, Georgia
Open Books	Chicago, Illinois
Politics and Prose	Chevy Chase, Washington DC
Writer's Block Bookstore	Winter Park, Florida
Yellow Book Road	San Diego, California

The important message here is: **Read books together.**

Pop reading to Natalie

Go on a city carriage ride

Cities such as New York, Chicago, New Orleans, Charleston, and Savannah all have carriage rides. Some cities have tram tours or Hop On, Hop Off trollies. Since they include narration about the history of the city, they are a great way to learn about an area.

Georgetown, SC tram tour

Visit a pumpkin patch

Arrange a special day out to pick out a pumpkin or visit a haunted house or hay maze. These are great Halloween activities. You can decorate your pumpkin when you get home. Stencils and stickers are available if you prefer to avoid carving.

Natalie visits a pumpkin patch

Attend a school fair

If the school your grandchildren attend has a yearly fair, it would be fun to attend together. As a matter of fact, it does not necessarily have to be their school but could be one in your neighborhood. These fairs are fun, and they help out local schools because they are fund-raisers.

Visit a fire station

Sofie, Andrew, PQ with fireman

Fire trucks are magnets for kids. Jana's local station even has wave runners for water rescues.

Call ahead and set up an appointment. When Jana and her grandchildren visited, the firemen were wonderful and gave the kids coloring books and some stickers. Be sure to take cookies as a gift. Have your grandchild(ren) help you make your favorite cookie recipe (or use the brownie recipe on page 23). They will be proud, and the firemen will appreciate their effort.

Take a Christmas lights tour

This is a nice way to have all the (local) kids on an outing together.   Follow up with some hot chocolate. Check out christmaslightfinder.com to find great displays.

Katie Michelle, and Natalie

Logan, Emilie, and Nick

Liz and Katie

Go garage sale shopping

Take one or two grandkids on a garage sale shopping spree. Give them a small amount of money and let them decide what/if to buy. Kids get a kick out of buying something fun/odd for not much money – and making their own decision.

Take a trip to a dollar store

Like garage sales, a visit to a Dollar Store allows kids to make the difficult choice of how to spend their dollar(s). Determine their spending allowance before you go.

Go to an arcade

Warning: a trip to the arcade can get expensive, and the process of choosing a prize can be lengthy.

See a movie at a theatre

It's still fun to see a movie on a big screen And, of course, popcorn and/or candy makes it special. Remember: no popcorn for the littlest ones. Be sure to comply with parental guidelines for movies.

Go to a museum

Goodness....the list here is endless. In Chicago, go to the Museum of Science and Industry, the Chicago History Museum, the Shedd Aquarium, the Museum of Natural History, or the Children's Museum at Navy Pier. In New Orleans, DO NOT MISS THE INSECTARIUM. REALLY! Their Children's Museum is also excellent for the younger crowd. Check out recommendations for your city or the city you want to visit.

Logan at City Museum, St. Louis, MO

Nick on the high wire in Kansas City, MO

Go bowling

Even young children can enjoy this family activity. Some bowling alleys have special racks so young children can roll their ball down the lane.

Natalie

Go to a water park

This is a fun activity for a hot day. Most parks have appropriate areas for children of all ages. Be sure you have enough adult supervision.

Go to the circus

Lynn and Jana recommend a compassionate, animal free circus. They have all the thrills and fun that you expect---without any animal cruelty.   There are talented trapeze artists, jugglers, clowns, etc.

Here is a partial list:

Bindlestiff Family Circus	Travels the world
Pickle Family Circus	Bay Area
Midnight Circus in the Park	Chicago
Cirque Italia	Traveling circus
Circus Luminous	Santa Fe
Cirque Eloize	Quebec
Cirque Plume	France
Flying High Circus	Tallahassee, Florida
Swamp Circus	Penryn, England
The 7 Fingers	Traveling circus
Circus Vargas	Traveling circus based in San Diego

Attend a live theatre presentation

High school and local college plays count! Some of them are fabulous AND MUCH CHEAPER than Broadway. Community theatre can be fun, too.

Logan and Nick at Lindenwood College Theater

Go to a zoo

If you don't have one nearby, this activity is worth a special trip.

Go to a petting zoo

Also try a butterfly garden.
(It's a great photo op, too).

Logan in the birdcage at the St. Louis Zoo

Take a train ride

This could be at a permanent location, such as Tweetsie Railroad in North Carolina, or a scheduled trip between two locations.

BEST RAILROAD TRIP EVER: The POLAR EXPRESS. Due to the popularity of the book and movie, railroads began adding this seasonal trip. This is a listing of states I have found that offer a Christmas train trip. Check out the one nearest to you and make reservations EARLY as they sell out fast.

Alabama
Arizona
Arkansas
California
Colorado
Connecticut
Delaware
Florida
Georgia
Hawaii
Illinois
Louisiana
Maryland
Missouri
Nevada
New Jersey
New York
North Carolina
Ohio
Texas
Washington
West Virginia
Wisconsin

Attend a camp

There are some camps, such as a YMCA camp, that include adults and children.

Nick getting face painted at Camp　　*Nick and Logan at Camp Craft room*

Attend a cooking class

Classes are often offered at high-end grocery stores or kitchen supply stores.

Attend a class at a craft store

Michaels', Lowe's Hardware Store and Home Depot offer craft events. One Saturday, you could build a birdhouse. Check with your local store for what is available and their schedule.

Go on a hot air balloon ride

This could be exciting for older kids who are tall enough to see over the basket. Be sure to get parental permission.

Take a helicopter ride

This would be a thrill for kids of all ages--grandparents included.

Go horseback riding

Kids like this, but it can be rough on a grandparent who does not normally ride a horse. Be sure you won't get saddle sores before you offer this one. Guided tours look after the kids, but it would be nice to do it with them if you are able.

Hire a limo

Forty years ago, Jana's husband hired a limo to drive their family across the Golden Gate Bridge. She thought it was terribly extravagant, but they did not have a car on that vacation, and their children STILL remember driving across the bridge, licking their ice cream cones in the fancy long car.

A few years ago, she went to New Orleans with her daughter and two of her children. She was the "nanny" while her daughter attended a conference. Though they walked and took the St. Charles trolley nearly everywhere they went, she hired a driver through a local limo service to take them on an afternoon sightseeing trip to see areas where they could not easily travel. That way, the car seat stayed in the car with the driver while they made a couple of stops, and they could see areas of the city that they would have missed.

Go to an escape room

Be sure to find one that is family friendly. An escape room that has a live zombie whose chains keep releasing through the hour may not be a good choice for your group. The room Jana and her family chose had a limit of 10 people, but there were 12 of them, including a 4 year old and a 6 year old. When she called ahead, the owner okayed their extra numbers and didn't even charge them for the two young ones. You can imagine her excitement when the 6 year old figured out how to get an important clue out of a barrel.

Lucille, 2017

Volunteer together

There are many creative ways to volunteer based on local needs and your grandchild's interests. Be advised some organizations have a required minimum age – call first.

For more information and ideas go to websitehttps://lauragrace weldon.com/2013/06/27/40-ways-kids-can-volunteer-toddler-to-teen/

Here is a sampling of opportunities to help a young person lay a foundation for volunteer work:

Make a "grandfriend"

If you have local grandchildren, escort them to regularly visit a "grandfriend" at a nursing home, assisted living facility, or in the neighborhood. Play card games, do crafts together, exchange advice, and build a connection. Check to see if a facility near you has programs in place.

Write to soldiers

Write letters to deployed service members.

There are many web sites to help you decide who to write to and what to write. You can also take letters to your local National Guard Armory and have them forward them as needed.

Write thank you notes

Have little ones draw special pictures. Use these along with a note like "thanks for being so nice" or "you made my day." Then stay on the lookout for a nice cashier, helpful librarian, or kind friend and let the grandchild hand out a surprise note. This activity can help kids see and appreciate people. Mr. Rogers always stressed that his mother told him in times of trouble, look for the helpers. That can be comforting when children hear terrible things on the news.

Work at a "soup kitchen" or food pantry

See if there is a local organization that serves free meals. Check if you can help. Perhaps you could sign up to set tables, help cook, serve beverages, and/or clean up. If not, you can collect canned foods or funds from neighbors to donate to a food pantry.

Say thank you to local policemen and women

Make cookies and deliver them to your local police or fire station. Make cut out cookies (see page 16) or just buy ready to bake cookie dough for making quick and easy cookies. Amazon offers a variety of badge shaped cookie cutters.

Help out at a pet shelter

Shelters often have age restrictions for volunteers. Call first before you suggest it so that kids won't be disappointed. Most shelters need dog walkers, and many have programs for kids to come read to their dogs. Another option is to gather up your no-sew dog toys (refer to page 37) and take them to the local shelter. Shelters will appreciate donations of pet food, blankets, towels, and newspapers.

Overnight Excursions

Visit the ever-popular Disney Land/World

Nick, Donald, and Logan

Logan and Nick in Epcot Center

Though these are popular destinations, there are many other great places to visit. There are several web sites that have lists of recommended places to go with kids in the US. They would be great excursions if you are lucky enough to live near by. If you are thinking of a big trip, you could consider one or more of them.

Suggested list:

1. Yellowstone National Park	Wyoming/Montana/Idaho
2. U.S. Space and Rocket Center	Huntsville, Alabama
3. Grand Canyon National Park	Northwestern Arizona
4. One World Trade Center	New York, New York
5. City Museum	St. Louis, Missouri
6. Yosemite National Park	Mariposa, California
7. Schlitterbahn Waterpark	New Braunfels, Texas
8. Arches National Park	Moab, Utah
9. Cedar Point	Sandusky, Ohio
10. Musical Instrument Museum	Phoenix, Arizona
11. Alcatraz Island	San Francisco, California
12. National Air and Space Museum	Washington, DC
13. Georgia Aquarium	Atlanta, Georgia
14. Freedom Trail	Boston, Massachusetts
15. Sleeping Bear Dunes	Empire, Michigan
16. Dinosaur Valley State Park	Glen Rose, Texas
17. Middleton Place	Charleston, South Carolina
18. Everglades National Park	South Florida
19. Art Institute of Chicago	Chicago, Illinois
20. Mammoth Cave National Park	South Central Kentucky
21. Heartland Harvest Garden	Kansas City, Missouri
22. Dinosaur Valley State Park	Fort Worth, Texas
23. NASCAR Hall of Fame	Charlotte, NC.
24. Denali National Park and Preserve	Denali, Alaska
25. San Antonio River Walk	San Antonio, Texas
26. The French Quarter	New Orleans, Louisiana
27. Statue of Liberty and Ellis Island	New York, New York
28. Rock & Roll Hall of Fame	Cleveland, Ohio
29. National Civil Rights Museum	Memphis, Tennessee

30. Niagara Falls	New York & Ontario, Canada
31. Six Flags	multiple sites US and Canada
32. Busch Gardens	Tampa, Florida
33. Cedar Point	Sandusky, Ohio
34. Hershey Park	Hershey, Pennsylvania
35. Colonial Williamsburg	Williamsburg, Virginia
36. Strawberry Banke	Portsmouth, New Hampshire

You can find many more ideas for fun and educational adventures at http://www.parents-choice.org/adventures.cfm. This Family Adventure site allows you to click on your state for an inclusive list of family friendly venues and events in your area.

Go to sleep-over camp

Great Camp Sagamore (www.sagamore.org) in New York offers a 6 day Grands Camp. Or attend a music camp with your grandchild who plays an instrument. That would free up a parent to spend time with other children in the family....or just go to work without guilt.

Host your own camp

Grandparents call their camps Camp Nana, Cousins Camp, Camp (your first name). Your camp can be a day camp or an overnight camp. For some great ideas, buy *Cousins Camp 2.0*. It is available on Amazon and bookstores. There are multiple ideas on how to host a camp for your grandchildren. After six years with children only in attendance, Jana's camp morphed into a family camp for the last four years. Though the activities are still geared toward the children, the parents come, too.

Take a trip without the parents

Jana's mother took her children on trips when they turned 10. Paul and Jana have taken grandchildren to Disney World and on a Disney Cruise. Lynn has ventured out to Kansas City and Disney World with her two grandsons.

Be sure to plan a DETAILED itinerary so that all the information you might need is at your fingertips. This will make your trip go smoothly.

Lynn's list for her Kansas City trip:

Kansas City Trip Oct 24-26, 2014

Friday Oct 24
KC weather: 81-59 sunny
3:00 PM   Leave for train departure station with boys
4:30   Amtrak departs to KC
           Train # 313: Kirkwood, Mo –
           Kansas City, Mo
           Depart 4:29 PM, Friday, October 24, 2014
           #8AA5XX. e tickets
           Eat dinner on train.
           Take additional snacks
9:20   Arrive KC, taxi to hotel
10:00   Hotel la Quinta in north KC
           (close to where we are visiting)
           guaranteed late arrival conf#318999
           Address: 2214 Taney Street,
           Kansas City, MO 64116 (816) 221-1200

Sat Oct 25

8:00 AM   Rise and eat breakfast at hotel
9:30   Taxi to Hallmark visitor center
              Opens at 9:30. Take tour
              2501 McGee St. - View Map
10:30   Walk to Legoland (entry not until 11AM)
11:00   Entry to Legoland.
              Conf 128140999 (will provide entry to Legoland)
              Pickup tickets for Sea Life for Sunday
              Spend rest of day in Legoland
              (No re-entry into Legoland - done once we leave)

Logan on Kansas City trip

Some travel companies have exclusive trips for families or grandparents traveling with a grandchild: check out Road Scholars, Classic Journeys, Grandtravel, Elderhostel, Sierra Club. Traveling with a tour group can make planning easier. An added bonus could be new friendships for you and your grandchild.

IMPORTANT NOTE:

Be sure to have important insurance and medication information with you if you are traveling out of your city or state. Have the parents sign a Permission to Seek Medical Care form. Make sure you have any appropriate medications and directions for use. Though parents may be easily available through cell phones and messaging, it is still a good idea to be prepared.

"Grandpa, can your inner child come out and play?"

Web Sites to Help You Plan

As you continue your planning, there are lots of websites to check out:

http://pbskids.org/zoom/activities/games/ This site divides games into categories, such as relay races, physical challenges, chase games, mind games, sports games, word games.

Crayola.com This site includes a section for coloring and crafts as well as a shopping area for Crayola products.

https://www.thespruce.com You will find the top science web sites for kids here. You can find out how stuff works, visit the Exploratorium in San Francisco, make a lava-filled volcano, and more.

https://curiousworld.com You can sign up for a free trial. The site provides games, videos, and books for children aged 2-7.

www.nationalgeographic.com There are games, videos, lots of information about animals.

ABCmouse.com. This site provides a full online curriculum for children aged 2-8. They allow you to try it free for 30 days and claim to have over 8,500 activities.

www.funbrain-games.eu This is another site that allows free access for a limited time. It has curriculum through 8th grade and tracks the student's progress, making the problems increasingly more difficult.

gws.ala.org This site is sponsored by the Association for Library Service to Children. It includes a site of the week and sections on history, math, computers, literature, animals, and the arts.

spatulatta.com This is a cooking site for kids. It includes healthy recipes and great how-to directions. It makes clear which steps should be completed by an adult.

http://www.parents-choice.org/adventures.cfm This site has an interactive map that will help you plan day trips or road trips. You will find children's museums, zoos, national parks, and points of interest in every state.

nwf.org Under the Family Fun section, you will find games, recipes, printables, songs, and contests.

***

Note: Any products or company names used throughout the book have not been solicited, and neither Jana nor Lynn has received any compensation for their use.

About the Authors

Jana and Lynn have been friends since they became randomly selected roommates at the University of Illinois in 1965. Since their early days together, they enjoyed documenting their activities:

They studied together:

And they played together:

Though Lynn has lived in Arizona, Illinois, and Missouri, and Jana has lived in Illinois, Michigan, and South Carolina, they have visited each other often and kept in touch for over 50 years! They and their husbands are now all retired.

Writing this book has allowed them to continue to play together.

***

Jana Dube Hletko

Jana Hletko and her pediatrician husband, Paul, have three married children and nine grandchildren. While Jana stayed home with their children when they were very young, she and her husband became interested in child car safety and helped get legislation passed in Michigan requiring the use of child car seats. She then worked for a community hospital in an education program to encourage seat belt and car seat use.

She is a creative educator, parent, and grandparent. She returned to teaching when they moved to South Carolina in 1989 and was one of the first 100 teachers in the United States to attain certification from the National Board of Professional Teaching Standards. In 1999-2000, she was the Georgetown County (SC) Teacher of the Year, and she was the South Carolina Journalism Teacher of the Year in 2005.

Though the Hletkos are fortunate to live by a beach in South Carolina (since 1989), their children have settled in Chicago and Washington, D.C. Jana and Paul have tried to spend as much quality time with their grandchildren as possible.

Her first book, *Cousins Camp*, has helped other grandparents enjoy the fun and excitement of planning and conducting their own Cousins Camp in order to spend special time with their grandchildren. That book was updated in 2017 (*Cousins Camp, 2.0*) to incorporate some of the new ideas in her camps.

Lynn Zacny Busby

Lynn Busby and her computer talented husband Bob have 4 children between them and 7 grandchildren.

Lynn and Bob owned and operated an Apple Computer Dealership in the early days of personal computing. Both spent their careers in the computer business and worked for large corporations including Toshiba, IBM, and MasterCard. They helped Paul and Jana through the pains and pangs of becoming computer literate.

The Busbys are fortunate to have their children and grandchildren near by. Over the years, they have spent countless hours in quality time with their grandchildren. They have babysat, vacationed together, and have been able to share birthdays and holidays. They have developed many family traditions that their grandchildren will always remember.

Lynn has been tracing her maternal grandfather's history and is working on a book to be published on Amazon that will be helpful to all DePriest descendents.

Lynn did all the technical work for Jana's first book and the revision as well. She was one of the friends who encouraged Jana to share what she had learned through her years of Cousins Camps. With her technical expertise, the book was published.

Made in the USA
Middletown, DE
16 September 2021